KU-390-708

Historical Characters **Julius Caesar**

Ruins of Caesar's Forum, in Rome.

Julius Caesar

Peter Muccini

Rupert Hart-Davis London

Granada Publishing Limited
First published in Great Britain 1972 by
Rupert Hart-Davis Educational Publications
3 Upper James Street, London, WIR 4BP

HARINGEY SCHOOL LIBRARY SERVICE

| 10/73 GRS 75p | 79 | |

Copyright © 1972 by McGraw-Hill Far Eastern Publishers (S) Ltd.

All rights reserved. No part of this book may be reprinted, or reproduced or utilized in any form or by any electronic, mechanical or other means, now known or hereafter invented, including photocopying and recording, or in any information storage and retrieval system, without permission in writing from the Publisher.

ISBN 0 298 12011 9

Acknowledgements
The frontispiece and photographs facing page 1, on the back cover, and on pages 4, 8, 11, 12, 19, 25, 28, 29, 30, 33, 36, 39, 45, 49, 52, 55 and 56 are reproduced by courtesy of C.E.I. Milan. The photograph on page 2 is reproduced by courtesy of Foto Parisio, Naples; on page 6 by courtesy of Blackhawk Films, Iowa, and on page 17 by courtesy of Robert Emmett Bright, Rapho Guillumette. The photograph on page 21 is reproduced by courtesy of Italian National Tourist Bureau; on page 47 (a) by courtesy of the British Museum, and on page 47 (b) by courtesy of Louvre Archives Photographiques.

BACK COVER: The *Forum Romanum* contained many of Rome's most important buildings, and was the centre of the city's life.

Printed and bound in Singapore by McGraw-Hill Far Eastern Publishers (S) Ltd.

CONTENTS

Bust of Caesar in the Capitoline Museum, Rome.

The Young Soldier

The streets of ancient Rome seethed with excitement. The great general, Lucius Cornelius Sulla, was returning with his victorious army from Asia Minor. Sulla had defeated Mithridates, a fierce and stubborn foe of the Romans, who had been slaughtering Roman citizens in Greece. The rulers of Rome were very grateful to Sulla and they had decided to give him a triumph.

Lucius Cornelius Sulla (138–78 B.C.) made himself dictator of Rome in 82 B.C.

A triumph was always a wonderful occasion. It was a parade, a carnival, and a public holiday rolled into one. For the poor people of the city it meant days of free feasting and drinking. In the great stadiums of the city there were games and chariot races, and fights to the death between men and men, and between men and wild beasts.

The parade itself would be heralded by a fanfare of trumpets and the beating of drums. Hundreds of chariots, pulled by prancing steeds, rumbled past. Thousands of soldiers, laden with plunder taken from the enemy, marched past the magnificent buildings with their soaring roofs and splendid white columns. Shambling miserably behind all the pomp and glory came the prisoners of war, captured in battle. They were doomed to a life of slavery under Roman masters.

Sometimes the parades would include strange new animals, such as elephants and camels, and the people would stare in wonder as these creatures were led past. Throughout it all, the people cheered themselves hoarse. At times like these even the poorest Roman swelled with pride at being the citizen of such a powerful state.

But there was one young man in the crowd that day who was not very happy to see Sulla returning to Rome in triumph. The young man was Gaius Julius Caesar. He was slight in build and had reddish hair. He came from a very old family which claimed the goddess Venus as one of its ancestors.

1

Venus, the Roman goddess
of love and beauty. Caesar's
family claimed her as an
ancestress. Many Roman
families believed themselves
descended from the great
figures of mythology.

Because the Caesar family was noble it was known as a *patrician* family. But many members of the family had for a long time believed that the true strength of Rome lay not with the proud and wealthy patricians, but with the ordinary people, the *plebeians*. The plebeians had built up the city from a tiny farming village, almost a thousand years before the birth of Christ, into one of the most powerful states on earth.

Caesar's family had allied itself with the plebeians. Caesar's aunt, Julia, had married a plebeian leader named Gaius Marius, a man whose ancestors had been simple farmers. Marius proved himself to be a great leader. He successfully defended Rome against the attacks of barbarians and created a powerful army. Caesar admired his uncle and modelled his own life on him. Caesar had married a girl called Cornelia when he was 16. In those days people of important families married young to form alliances. Cornelia was the daughter of Cinna, another plebeian who had helped Marius rule Rome. But Marius and Cinna were now dead. Caesar's father had also died and the young man in the cheering crowd felt defenceless. He had good reason to be afraid. Sulla, the patrician, hated the plebeians. He was determined to destroy them and become dictator of Rome. Most of all, he hated the Caesar family.

Gaius Marius (157–86 B.C.), a successful general and a leader of the plebeians, was married to Caesar's aunt. Marius and Sulla were political rivals.

Caesar's fears were soon proved right. After his triumph, Sulla became dictator of Rome and began to hunt down and slay his plebeian enemies. Many were murdered and others went into hiding. Caesar waited in dread, wondering when he would be arrested. One day a messenger from Sulla came to his house.

'If you are loyal to Sulla,' the messenger said, 'you will divorce your wife Cornelia and show that you are no longer a friend of the plebeians.'

Caesar knew that if he refused to obey Sulla's command he would probably be put to death. Other people who had been ordered by Sulla to divorce their wives had obeyed promptly. One of them

Marcus Tullius Cicero (106–43 B.C.), famous as a writer and statesman, was also an orator of great skill and power.

had been Cicero, who was one of the most renowned of Roman orators and politicians.

But Caesar refused to obey. Proudly and angrily he told the messenger: 'Go tell your master that I shall never give up my wife — for him or for any man.'

When Sulla received Caesar's reply he sent out spies and soldiers to arrest this defiant young man. Friends hurriedly warned Caesar of the great danger he faced and Caesar went into hiding in the hilly region north-east of Rome.

He had to keep on the move all the time. He slept by day on the ground and travelled by night. It was a time of great hardship. All the time the enemy was close at hand. One night, one of Sulla's patrols caught him by surprise. Caesar bribed the captain of the patrol and managed to escape.

But things became desperate. Caesar even thought of leaving Rome to live as an exile in a distant land. To make matters worse he became quite ill and had to be carried on a stretcher.

One day a friend came to see him at one of his hiding places.

'We are pleading with Sulla for you in Rome,' the friend said. 'I think it is safe for you to come back.'

Caesar pondered on the problem. He was tired and ill. He knew he could not go on as a fugitive. He was certain to be caught one day and then he would surely be put to death. He decided to take a chance and returned to Rome. There Cornelia nursed him back to health.

The day came when Caesar had to go to Sulla and ask for pardon. Caesar's friends went on ahead of him to plead his cause.

'Oh, Sulla!' they said, 'we beg you to forgive Caesar for disobeying you. He did not mean any disloyalty. He is a hot-headed young man who does not understand these matters. He loves his wife dearly and does not want to be separated from her. He means you no harm and does not want to interfere in the affairs of the city.'

Meanwhile Caesar made his way to the Forum, where Sulla sat listening to the pleas. The Forum was the heart of ancient Rome. It was a familiar sight to Caesar. His parents had taken him there often as a boy to hear the great speakers address the crowds.

The Forum was a hive of activity. There was a two-storey market

Ruins of the *Forum Romanum* (Roman Forum), the heart of Rome in Caesar's time. The Forum included temples, courts, assembly rooms, markets, the meeting place of the Senate, and the public record office.

in one of the gleaming white marble buildings. Shoppers set up a great hubbub as they haggled with the merchants over the goods on display. Along the pavements men sat drinking wine and gambling with dice. All around stood beautiful buildings, such as the temple of Saturn and the temple of Castor and Pollux with its magnificent columns. Down the middle of the Forum ran the *Via Sacra* — the Sacred Way — which led to the house of the High Priest of Rome.

Sulla sat silently listening to the pleas. By this time young Caesar had arrived and he stood in front of the dictator. The two men gazed at one another for a time. Then Sulla slowly raised his hand in an act of pardon.

'You have made your point and you can have him,' he declared. Then he added sharply: 'But remember . . . one Caesar is worse than a dozen Mariuses.'

Caesar could hardly believe his luck. He had been spared. It was an extremely important moment for Rome. Young Caesar was to become the greatest Roman of them all. Not only did he distinguish himself as a soldier, a statesman, a lawmaker, and a writer, but he helped Rome to become the most powerful state on earth. It was an empire that was later to stretch from the wet and windy shores of the Atlantic Ocean in the west to the hot deserts of western Asia in the east; from the cold, damp forests of Germany in the north to the burning sands of the deserts of northern Africa in the south. Throughout this vast region the name of Caesar would be known, feared, and respected.

But in the meantime, Caesar was still a young man in a rather weak position. It was not safe for him to stay in Rome even though Sulla had pardoned him. The Caesar family had too many enemies and Sulla might change his mind. In 81 B.C., when Caesar was only 19, he set out for Asia Minor to fight the rebellious Mytileneans, allies of the troublesome Mithridates.

Caesar took part in the attack on the city of Mytilene, which fell to the Romans. During the battle Caesar distinguished himself by saving the life of one of his soldiers. The exploit brought him his first military decoration — a crown of oak leaves, which marked him out as a hero.

After the victory Caesar sailed back to Rome to Cornelia and his baby daughter. He was now 22 years old. His ambitions for power began to grow, but Sulla was still dictator. The plebeian party, which

Caesar wanted to join, was divided and confused. Caesar did not want to take sides in their quarrels so he lived as a private citizen, writing poetry to pass the time, and giving parties which got him into debt.

Despite his idle life, Caesar never lost the desire to enter politics and become a powerful man in his great city. However, it could prove dangerous for him to do so. Sulla might forget he had pardoned

Ruins of the temple of Saturn, in the *Forum Romanum*.

Mithridates the Great (120–63 B.C.), king of Pontus. Contemporary head, showing him as Hercules. (Louvre, Paris)

him and have him killed. But there was one way in which Caesar could win the notice of the people: by going to law.

At that time there was a man called Gnaeus Dolabella who had served as an official under Sulla. Dolabella was a greedy and dishonest man. He had taken public money collected in taxes from the people and kept it for himself. Caesar accused Dolabella and exposed him in a court of law. Caesar's speech was a very good one and aroused great attention. Luckily for Dolabella, he had engaged the best lawyers in Rome, and Caesar lost the case. But Caesar had made his mark. Some time later, certain Greek citizens engaged Caesar to prosecute another of Sulla's officials. The Greeks claimed that this man had plundered their cities during the war against Mithridates. Caesar succeeded in obtaining a verdict of guilty against the man. However, powerful friends of the accused, working behind the scenes, had the verdict reversed. Caesar lost again, but once more he had made his mark.

Those two cases gave Caesar a taste for the law. He decided to go to the island of Rhodes in the eastern Mediterranean. There was a famous teacher on the island who instructed pupils in law and in *oratory*, or public speaking.

As Caesar's ship neared the coast of Asia Minor, a fleet of pirates waylaid the vessel. Caesar and the crew were taken prisoner. The pirates soon learned that they had an important prisoner on their hands. They promptly sent off a ransom note to Rome demanding 20 talents for his release. This was a large sum of money, equivalent to more than £10,000 today.

According to Plutarch, the great biographer of ancient times, Caesar was extremely angry when he heard the pirates had asked for that amount of money.

'It's not enough!' he cried. 'I am worth far more than that. You must ask for at least 50.'

The pirates gleefully increased their original demand and for the next five or six weeks they waited for the money to come. Plutarch wrote that during this time Caesar wrote poetry and read it to his captors. They were a rough lot and laughed at him. Caesar would then lose his temper at their jeering and shout at them: 'You are nothing but a bunch of stupid barbarians and I shall have you all put to death.'

The pirates thought this extremely funny and fell about laughing; and the young Roman would mutter: 'Just you wait and see.'

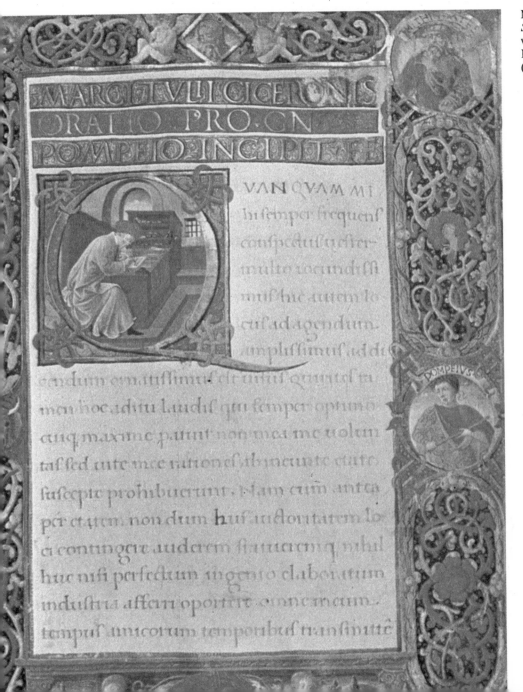

MARCI TVLII CICERONIS
ORATIO PRO CN
POMPEIO INCIPIT

VAN QVAM MI
hi semper frequens
conspectus uester
multo iocundissi
mus hic autem lo
cus ad agendum
amplissimus addi
cendum ornatissimus est tamen hoc aditu laudis qui semper optimo
cuique maxime patuit non mea me uolun
tas sed meae uitae rationes ab ineunte aetate
suscepte prohibuerunt. Nam cum antea
per aetatem non dum huis auctoritatem lo
ci contingere auderem statueremq nihil
huc nisi perfectum ingenio elaboratum
industria afferri oporteret omne meum
tempus amicorum temporibus transmitte

Medieval edition of Cicero's *Speech on Behalf of Pompey*, with marginal illustrations of Mithridates and Pompey. (National Library, Florence)

The ransom money came and the pirates released Caesar. He immediately went to some neighbouring towns and raised a band of fighting men.

'If you help me capture these pirates, you can have all the ransom money for yourselves,' he said.

For the first time in his military career, Caesar showed his two great gifts in attack: speed and surprise. Before they knew where they were the pirates had been overcome and captured. This time there was nothing for them to laugh about. Caesar had them all executed.

After this interlude Caesar went to Rhodes to take up his studies. Shortly afterwards, Mithridates broke the promise he had made to the Romans and went on the rampage once more. Caesar hurried over to Asia Minor and joined the Roman troops. It was during this campaign that he received word from his mother in Rome that her brother had died. Caesar's uncle had been a member of the College of Priests and Caesar was told the vacant seat was now his.

Relief on a Roman tomb, showing Roman cavalry in action during a campaign. (National Museum, Rome)

This was good news. A priest in ancient Rome was quite an important political official. As he set out for Rome in 74 B.C. at the age of 26, Caesar's hopes of a political career soared.

12

The Political Arena

What was the government of Rome like at that time?

Rome had been a republic since 509 B.C. In that year the people had risen against their king, proud Tarquin, and hurled him to his death from a lofty black crag that was afterwards known as Tarquin's Rock.

Tarquin was an Etruscan. He came from that region which now forms part of Tuscany. It had achieved a great civilization long before the Romans, and it had conquered Rome. Tarquin proved to be an oppressor. The Romans vowed that never again would they have a king to rule them. They decided instead to share the powers of government among the people by setting up a republic.

When Caesar returned to Rome from Asia Minor in 74 B.C. to take his seat in the College of Priests, Rome was still a republic. Sulla was a dictator, but dictators did not rule for very long. Sulla himself suddenly gave up power in 68 B.C. By then a great general named Pompey had won the support of the people and Sulla probably feared him.

The real framework of Rome's government lay with seven groups elected by the citizens. The Senate was the chief law-making body. In Caesar's day it had 600 members. These came mainly from the patrician class. The Senate house was called the *curia*. It stood in the Forum before a courtyard called the *comitium*. The ordinary people gathered in the comitium and held their own assembly there. This combination of the patricians and the plebeians formed the basic government of Rome. It was a combination expressed in the letters SPQR which appeared on public buildings and banners. The letters stood for SENATUS POPULUSQUE ROMANUS, meaning THE SENATE AND THE PEOPLE OF ROME. The Senate was responsible for all the important laws regarding finance and foreign

Model of an Etruscan soldier. The Etruscans were considered to be among the fiercest fighters in the Roman legions.

13

Ruins of a Roman villa. Many of the villas of the patricians were built in the styles of Ancient Greece, with balconies, terraces, statues, and gardens.

policy. However, the Tribunes, who represented the ordinary people in the Senate, could veto or cancel any law they disagreed with.

Two Censors selected candidates for election to the Senate. These two officials also carried out a regular *census*, in which the inhabitants of Rome were counted. The Censors were elected every five years for a term of office lasting 18 months.

Two Consuls were elected every year to serve for a year. The Consuls commanded the armed forces and presided over the Senate. They also introduced the laws debated in the Senate, and supervised the elections. Each Consul could veto any decision of the other if he disagreed with it. The Consuls were chief executives, rather like the president of the United States or of France today. The Consuls were represented throughout the Roman provinces by Proconsuls.

Eight Praetors were elected every year to serve for a year. These officials were responsible for the courts of justice. They also acted on behalf of the Consuls whenever the Consuls were away from Rome. The Praetors were represented in the provinces by Propraetors.

Twenty Quaestors were elected every year to serve for one year. Their task was to help the Consuls, the Praetors, and the provincial governors, mainly in money matters.

The Tribunes represented the common people in the Senate. Only plebeians could be Tribunes, and they, too, were elected every year to serve for one year. The Tribunes could veto any law passed in the Senate. They could also pass their own laws by calling a people's assembly.

Four Aediles supervised the markets, traffic, the organization of games, fire-fighting services, and other matters regarding the day-to-day running of the city. The Aediles were also elected every year to serve for one year.

The High Priest had no political functions. But he was appointed for life and he wielded considerable influence on the government.

Senior government officials were accompanied wherever they went by attendants known as Lictors. The Lictors' badge of office was a bundle of rods enclosing axes and bound together with thongs. These bundles were known as *fasces* and represented the authority of the state. The modern word *fascism*, meaning a dictatorial type of government, originated from these symbols. In olden days the Lictors used the rods to drive away anyone who got in the way of government officials as they walked through the streets. Consuls were accompanied by twelve Lictors, and Praetors by two.

In this way the government of Rome represented the two classes of the state: the patricians and the plebeians. These two groups had often clashed, sometimes with terrible bloodshed. Marius and Sulla had fought against each other. When Caesar joined the College of Priests, Rome was having a period of comparative peace. The patricians were in the minority, but because of their great wealth and the electoral system which worked in their favour, they held the upper hand.

Free Roman citizens paid no taxes. The city lived on the great wealth that poured in from conquered lands. The patricians lived in magnificent villas set in splendid gardens decorated with beautiful statues and sparkling fountains. They often gave lavish banquets consisting of many courses. They ate such delicacies as larks' tongues, and mice cooked in honey. All the work was done by slaves captured in war. The slaves looked after the children, did the washing, cooked, and carried out all the other humble tasks. But some slaves were important. These included secretaries, librarians, and doctors. A few of these slaves were better off than many free Roman citizens.

The vast majority of Roman citizens could not afford to buy slaves or support them. Poor Romans lived in dingy old tenements, crowded together several to a room. Their food was very plain: rough bread, olives, a porridge made of ground wheat, and a few vegetables. On public holidays, during triumphs, or when the

The fasces, shown on a coin of Caesar's time, symbolized the authority of Rome.

15

Roman chariots. (Above) *Biga*, pulled by two horses. (Below) *Quadriga*, pulled by four.

patricians wanted to win the support of the masses in elections, the common people would be given meat and wine at banquets.

The one bright spot in the life of the poor was the games. They matched the excitement of football matches, boxing, or motor-racing today. But the Roman games were extremely cruel. Men known as *gladiators* fought each other to the death in the arenas before thousands of howling spectators. Perhaps the most popular sport was chariot-racing. Chariots pulled by two horses, were known as *bigae*. Those with three horses were called *trigae*, and those with four horses, *quadrigae*.

The master of the games sat on a raised platform in the centre of the arena. He started the race by raising his arm and the chariots charged round the arena seven times. Often there were spectacular crashes as the chariots ran into each other at bends or while thundering down the strait. Wheels came off and charioteers would be hurled high into the air to land amid the grinding wheels and the flailing hooves.

Caesar entered politics as a firm supporter of the plebeian party. He was ambitious, and aimed for the top of the system. His first stepping stone was the post of Aedile. With the help of an extremely rich Roman called Crassus, Caesar was elected Aedile in 65 B.C. He immediately set out to use his post to make himself popular with the common people. He decorated the streets and squares of Rome. He gave lavish banquets and presented plays in the theatres. But most of all he staged some of the most exciting games the city had ever known. He recruited so many gladiators that the patricians became alarmed. They were afraid he might use them to seize power in the city.

Caesar clad his gladiators in magnificent silver armour. The Roman people, who always loved a fine spectacle, were very impressed with this new Aedile.

Caesar's progress to power received a major push forward when

In the games that were the delight of the Roman populace, wild beasts were made to fight each other or to do battle with human beings. This fourth century mosaic shows a Roman gladiator killing a leopard. (Borghese Gallery, Rome)

the High Priest died. He immediately presented himself as a candidate for this high office. He spent a considerable sum of money on feasts and games to win the favour of the people. He knew he had to win the election. If he failed his whole political future would be ruined. On the day of his election he told his mother: 'Today you will see your son either made High Priest or in exile.'

When the result was announced Caesar had won by a large majority. The patricians became more uneasy. They remembered Sulla's words that one Caesar was more dangerous than a dozen Mariuses. Their fears grew in 62 B.C. when Caesar was elected Praetor. The new Praetor decided to try out his powers right away. He stood up in the Senate and accused Catulus, the leader of the law-making body, of misusing funds that should have been spent on repairing the temple of Saturn.

The patricians were furious. They all rushed to the Senate building and forced Caesar to drop the charge. Caesar did so but shortly afterwards he proposed a law to recall Pompey and his troops to Rome from abroad. The patricians saw even greater danger in this move. By this time Caesar's wife Cornelia had died and he had married Pompeia, a cousin of the great general.

'He will use Pompey and the army to seize power over all Rome,' the patricians cried.

The situation became tense. There were fights in the Forum between the supporters of Caesar and those of the patricians. The angry patricians then dismissed Caesar from his post of Praetor. This set off a riot. A mob of Caesar's supporters stormed the Senate and the terrified patricians were forced to reinstate Caesar.

After this episode Caesar did nothing. He had tested his powers and discovered that when it came to a showdown with the patricians, he could win. Shortly afterwards, in 61 B.C., he left for Spain and Portugal, where he conquered more territory for Rome and at the same time increased his fame.

Pompey the Great, Gnaeus Pompeius Magnus (106–48 B.C.), was at first Caesar's friend and ally. But later the two became bitter enemies.

Caesar returned to Rome in 60 B.C. with a long line of victories to his credit in Spain and Portugal. Each new conquest brought Rome more wealth in the tributes that the conquered people were forced to pay, rather like taxes. Caesar's defeat of the rebellious tribes in those distant lands overlooking the Atlantic Ocean had added new fame to his reputation. He easily won his election to the post of Consul. He had reached the top of the ladder, more or less. In his new post he commanded the Roman armed forces. He also had a big say in what laws were to be passed in the Senate.

But Caesar was not completely satisfied. The other Consul, Bibulus, was a patrician. Caesar's quarrel with this rich group had not ended with the riots in the Forum. He felt himself tied down and he immediately began to look for ways to increase his power. He chose two men as his allies. The first was Crassus, perhaps the wealthiest man in Rome. Crassus had helped Caesar become an Aedile, and he had quarrelled with the patrician senators. The other man was Pompey, who commanded a powerful army. Caesar had divorced his wife Pompeia, following a scandal she had become involved in. He now decided that he must re-establish his links with Pompey's family. He therefore married for a third time. His wife was Calpurnia, the daughter of one of Pompey's supporters.

Caesar, Crassus, and Pompey realized that together they made a very powerful team. Crassus had the money. Pompey had the military strength, and was popular as a hero among the people, while Caesar had the brains and the ambition. The three men came together and formed a *triumvirate*. This word comes from the Latin, and it means simply a group of three men. It was an extremely powerful trio. The triumvirate soon made it clear to the patricians that they would stand no opposition to their aims. Their greatest weapon was the threat of using physical force on anyone who tried to stop them.

One of the first things Caesar did as Consul was to change a Senate law appointing him director of forests in the provinces. The Senate had passed this law in an attempt to downgrade

The Appian Way, a paved
highway leading from Rome
to Brundisium. The Romans
were among the greatest road-
builders in history. Without a
developed system of highways,
they would have been unable
to rule their vast territories.

Alexander the Great (356–323 B.C.), one of the greatest of all conquerors. Caesar admired and also envied him.

him. It was not much of a position and carried no real authority with it. Caesar had taken it as an insult.

With the help of the plebeians, and with the pressure of the triumvirate, he had himself appointed as the responsible governor of Cisalpine Gaul. This was that region of Italy that ran south from the Alps to central Italy. Later, Caesar's dominion was extended to Transalpine Gaul, a region now including all of France and parts of Belgium.

Caesar's new position gave him five legions. This was a force of some 30,000 men. He also had the right to set up colonies throughout this vast region, and was responsible for Illyricum, most of which formed part of present-day Yugoslavia.

He had come a long way since that day when he had fearfully stood before Sulla with his life dangling by a thread. But there was much more to be done. Caesar's dreams of power were great. He was 40 years old and he remembered with some bitterness that Alexander the Great had conquered practically the entire known world by the age of 33, some three and a half centuries before.

Caesar felt that to reach great power he had to score some really spectacular military victories. He thought of Transalpine Gaul, with all its fierce tribes fighting each other to gain possession of its natural wealth, and of that misty land far to the west across that sea of which he had heard travellers speak; and he and his legions set out in 58 B.C. on his greatest adventure.

A World for Conquest

Caesar had proved himself a skilful politician in Rome. But Rome, great as it was, was only a city. Could he impose his rule on such a vast territory as Gaul? Scores of fierce tribes were just as anxious as he to conquer. The warlike Helvetii, a people who lived in a region which now includes part of Switzerland, were moving westwards from the Alps. Their aim was to cross the River Rhône, the great waterway that flows southwards into the Mediterranean.

In the north-west the enemy was the Belgae. In the north-east, the Germans, perhaps the most feared of all, lurked in their dark forests, from which they emerged from time to time to strike terror into the hearts of neighbouring tribes. Many people in Gaul regarded the Germans as invincible. These people were glad to see Caesar and his troops arrive. They looked upon the Romans as protectors, and many joined Caesar as allies.

Caesar spent nine years in his campaigns in Gaul. He fought many a bloody battle but he lost only two. At the end he succeeded in establishing the authority of Rome from the banks of the River Rhine to the English Channel. He also laid down the foundations for the Roman colonization of Britain that was to begin a hundred years later.

Throughout it all, his troops were utterly devoted and loyal to him, despite some isolated cases of hesitation. The soldiers respected him because he shared their own rough way of life. Wherever the battle was at its thickest, Caesar was there to encourage his men. He was a very brave man, but he never took foolish risks. When the situation became too dangerous or hopeless, Caesar was wise enough to retreat. He did not believe in useless heroic gestures.

The backbone of the Roman army was the legionary. The legionary was a foot soldier or infantryman. He was armed with two javelins measuring about 2·5 metres in length. The legionary could hurl a javelin to a distance of nearly 20 metres. For close, hand-to-hand fighting, the legionary was armed with a short, sharp sword. His head and face were protected by a metal helmet with side flaps. The upper part of his body was guarded by a tunic made of tough leather covered with overlapping metal scales resembling chain mail or armour.

The main food of the legionaries was wheat. The army was equipped with portable mills which ground the wheat grain into flour. The flour was then made into a kind of porridge. Every legionary cut his hair short. He also kept his face shaved. He carried his food in a pack strapped to his back. Heavier equipment was carried by pack animals.

A hundred legionaries formed a century. This combat unit was led by an officer called a centurion, equivalent to a captain in a modern army. Six centuries formed a cohort, and ten cohorts made up a legion numbering 6,000 men at full strength.

The army also had cavalry troops. These horsemen would gallop into battle and scatter the enemy after the legionaries had first attacked with their javelins and swords. Engineers dug trenches, built fortified camps, erected bridges across rivers, and operated the various machines used in battles. These machines included huge catapults that hurled rocks and other missiles at the enemy. They were rather like artillery in a modern army. There were also battering rams to break down the heavy wooden gates of towns; climbing ladders to scramble up walls; and tall towers on wheels which were pushed up to an enemy fortification for close range bombardment.

Each legionary carried a long shield that protected him from his chin to his ankles. During certain attacks, the legionaries

A model of a legionary depicts the steadiness and determination of the Roman soldier.

Battering-ram, as used by Roman armies to demolish gates, walls, and earthworks. (Model from the Museum of Roman Civilization, Rome)

would come together, place the shields over their backs and crawl forward towards the walls of a city. This manoeuvre was known as a *testudo*, or tortoise. It was rather like a primitive tank, only worked by manpower.

Caesar recruited most of his legionaries from the poorer people of Rome. They were paid wages, and signed on for military service for up to 20 years. Caesar also drew troops from other lands. Many of his cavalrymen came from Gaul and Germany. The soldiers who operated the catapults and slings came mainly from the Balearic Isles, off the eastern coast of Spain. Cretans and Egyptians served as archers. These foreigners served with Caesar because they wanted to become Roman citizens.

Caesar's first major test in Gaul came as a horde of almost 400,000 Helvetii gathered at the River Rhône. Caesar built fortifications on the banks of the river. His troops were heavily outnumbered, but he succeeded in pushing the invaders back. Meanwhile, he sent for reinforcements. After two weeks of

The Roman cavalry in action.

following the enemy army, the Roman legions began to run short of food. Caesar stopped pursuing the Helvetii and moved northwards to Bibracte, near where the present-day French town of Autun now stands.

The Helvetii thought Caesar had taken fright and was retreating. They launched an attack, confident that they would overcome the Romans. Caesar's army was on a hill. He drew up his troops in three lines across the middle of the slopes. He placed his more experienced soldiers near the front, and the younger ones nearer the summit. At the crest of the hill, hidden from view, the cavalry waited.

That morning Caesar made a stirring speech to his soldiers. He reminded them of the great victories they had already won and told them there could be no retreat. The Helvetii attacked just after noon. They were sure they could crush these thin lines of legionaries ranged on the hillside. But when they came close to the Romans they were met with a hail of javelins that devastated their ranks. Before the Helvetii could recover from the shock, Caesar ordered the next rank of his troops into the attack. The Romans advanced down the hillside, slashing with their swords to the right and left of them. The Helvetii retreated to another hill about a mile away to lick their wounds.

Shortly afterwards, the Helvetii remustered and sent a force of 15,000 men into battle. Caesar coolly brought his third line of men into action and soon the Helvetii had broken up and were fleeing for their lives. At about six in the evening, when the sun was beginning to set, the Roman cavalry galloped forth from behind the hilltop and put the finishing touches to the rout. The panic-stricken Helvetii were slaughtered as they ran. Those that survived, surrendered, and Caesar sent them back to their homeland.

Caesar's victory brought him great admiration from many

Gallic tribes. But it was only the first in a series of major battles. The next enemies were the Germans. They had crossed the Rhine and occupied a large part of eastern Gaul under the leadership of their king, Ariovistus. Stories of the fierceness and cruelty of the Germans were many. The Romans were filled with dismay. Caesar himself was reluctant to attack them. He tried at first to come to terms with them. He sent a delegation to Ariovistus but the German leader replied contemptuously: 'If I wanted anything from Caesar I would have gone to him; and if he wants anything from me he should come to me. This region of Gaul is mine by right of conquest.'

Caesar kept his temper. He was determined to try his hardest to avoid battle. He called on Ariovistus to withdraw from that

The Roman order of battle: the cavalry waited in readiness on the flanks until the legionaries had made the first assault on the enemy.

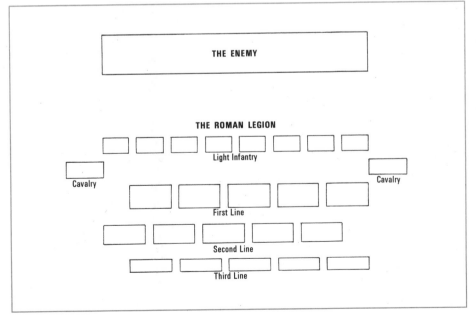

part of Gaul and to free the prisoners and hostages he had captured. Ariovistus refused. Instead, he marched on the town of Vesontio, which is present-day Besançon, near the Swiss border with France.

The Roman troops had become frightened. The soldiers went round telling each other stories they had heard about the enemy's savagery.

'They are so tough and warlike that some of them have not slept under a roof for fourteen years,' the soldiers whispered to each other.

The fear spread to the Roman officers. Some of them made excuses to go away. Others remained inside their tents and refused to come out.

Caesar angrily called his officers together and rebuked them sharply for their fears.

The Romans fighting the Gauls. (Detail from a mausoleum at St. Rémy, France)

'Why do you despair of your own courage and my competence?' he demanded angrily. 'We have fought this foe before under Gaius Marius and defeated them. They are the same enemy that the Helvetii have frequently fought and beaten, and yet the Helvetii proved no match for our army. Even Ariovistus himself knows that our army cannot be caught by tactics which he has used against unskilled barbarians.'

Looking scornfully at his officers Caesar continued: 'I intend to see whether honour or duty or cowardice prevails in your minds. Even if no one else follows I shall march with the Tenth Legion alone; I have no doubt of its allegiance.'

When Caesar finished his speech the officers rose shamefaced to their feet. They burst into cheers and swore their determination to fight and win. Those lessons in oratory Caesar had taken in Rhodes as a young man had served him well in a tight corner.

Caesar lined up his army about 24 km. from the Rhine in wait for Ariovistus and his troops: The Germans did not appear. Then

Caesar learned that the German leader was a very superstitious man. Fortune-tellers had predicted that he would be defeated if he engaged Caesar in battle before the new moon. So Ariovistus waited in his camp for the right time.

But Caesar was in no mood to wait, and he launched his attack. The fighting was bitter, but the Romans slowly gained the upper hand. At last the Germans were driven back towards the river. They were trapped, and the Roman cavalry had an easy task in killing them off. Ariovistus managed to escape across the Rhine, but the might of the Germans had been broken.

Gold coin, with Caesar's head, commemorating his victory over the Gauls.

Meanwhile the Belgae still controlled northern Gaul. As soon as the winter of 58–57 B.C. ended, Caesar marched his troops rapidly northwards, where the Belgae were waiting. They tried to encircle the Roman army, but Caesar used his archers and slingers to push them back. The Belgae retreated under the fury of the Roman onslaught, and they were harried by the Roman cavalry.

There was still a powerful group of enemies left. These were the Nervii, the fiercest group among the Belgae. One day, as the Romans were building a camp by the River Sambre, the Nervii launched a surprise attack. They rushed out of the wooded hills and caught the Romans completely unprepared. The Romans were scattered and helpless. Caesar showed his courage by rushing straight into the fray in an effort to get his men into some fighting order. When it seemed they were going to surrender he took up a shield and launched his own personal attack, calling on his men to follow. Caesar's action filled the Romans with new hope. But they were still heavily outnumbered. Just when it seemed too late, two legions of Caesar's rear-guard came rushing down the hill and struck at the Nervii. This time it was the enemy who was outnumbered. But the Nervii refused to surrender. They caught the Roman javelins as they whistled through the air and defiantly threw them back. When the battle ended with a Roman victory there were only

Bridge constructed by Caesar's army over the Rhine in 55B.C. (Model from the Museum of Roman Civilization, Rome)

500 left of the 60,000 Nervii who had commenced the fight.

After this victory most of Gaul was under Roman control. But there was always a rebellion somewhere. Caesar was kept busy dashing hither and thither stamping out these outbreaks. He even had to cross the Rhine because the Germans were beginning to raise an army to invade Gaul. Caesar was also fascinated by a land that lay only some 32 km. across the western sea. Sometimes, on an extremely clear day, its white cliffs could be seen gleaming faintly on the distant horizon. Caesar knew this land had become a refuge for rebellious Gauls who had escaped the clutches of his army. He knew that the people of that land had also helped the Gauls in their resistance to the Romans. He decided that this land, too, should be conquered. At the same time he was extremely curious to see a place which he had heard so much about from travellers. The island — for it was a great island on the edge of a huge ocean — was rich in metals such as tin and gold. Other peoples had invaded and settled there, so why not Caesar?

Guerrilla Warfare

Britain was the land Caesar planned to invade. The inhabitants were known as Britons. They belonged to various tribes. When they were not fighting one another they earned their living as farmers inland and as fishermen around the coasts. They lived in small villages, each consisting of a cluster of huts made of wooden poles and branches twisted together and covered in dried mud. The roofs of these huts were covered in reeds. At the top of the roof there was a hole to let out the smoke from the fire. There were no windows, so these huts were cold and draughty, and quite different from the magnificent villas of the Roman patricians.

The Britons dressed in brightly coloured clothes made of wool. The wives and daughters of the tribal chiefs wore necklaces and gold bracelets. Many of the Britons were descendants of invaders who had come hundreds of years before from countries such as Denmark, Norway, France, and Spain. Some of them crossed the Channel to trade with the Gauls.

In August 55 B.C. Caesar assembled a fleet to carry two legions across the sea. The ships left from a port near present-day Boulogne. Caesar knew that this was the closest point to Britain. Another fleet carrying the cavalry assembled at a nearby port and was to follow the rest.

As soon as there was a spell of fine weather, the Roman fleet set off. It was the middle of the night, and by early morning the invasion force saw land looming ahead of it. Tall white cliffs gleamed in the rising sun. On drawing close to the coast Caesar saw there was no suitable beach for landing. The cliffs rose sheer from the sea. Any waiting enemy at the top of them could have rained down rocks on intruders. Caesar sailed eastwards along the strange coast. Eventually they came to a place which had a flat beach, somewhere between the present-day towns of Walmer and Deal.

The Romans did not know it but they had been spotted by the Britons. Just as Caesar and his men were beginning to leave their galleys, the Britons suddenly appeared in chariots. The Roman soldiers soon found themselves in difficulties. The water was deeper than they thought and they were afraid to jump in and make their way to the shore. The Romans were also weighed down with their weapons and their packs. The Britons, on the other hand, knew the place well and had much greater freedom of movement. They rushed into the sea throwing missiles at the invaders and charging at them on horseback.

At this point Caesar ordered the big galleys to move up closer. The Britons had never seen such ships before. Their huge oars flashed in the sunlight and splashed through the waves. The prows reared up like the beaks of huge birds. The Britons were rather alarmed by it all. When the Romans brought out the artillery they had on board and sent huge rocks lobbing over towards the islanders, the Britons became even more flustered. But the Roman soldiers were flustered too and still hung back.

At that moment the standard bearer of the Romans, who carried a golden eagle on top of a metal rod, stood up on the prow of the ship and cried out: 'Leap down, soldiers, unless you wish to betray your eagle to the enemy. It shall be told that I at least did my duty to my country and general.'

Having said this, the standard bearer of the Tenth Legion leapt into the waves and began to move towards the enemy. On seeing this, the rest of the Roman soldiers took heart and followed him.

The battle that followed was fierce. The Britons cunningly waited until more Roman troops had entered the water and then sent in their cavalry to attack them as they floundered in the waves. Caesar's cavalry had not arrived. The ships carrying it had gone astray in

Julius Caesar. Copy of a contemporary statue. (Palazzo Senatorio, Rome)

33

the Channel. Gradually the iron discipline of the Romans came to the fore and the wild Britons were forced back.

However, Caesar soon discovered he had picked an awkward enemy to fight. Unlike the Helvetii and the Germans, who always rushed out in big numbers to do battle, the Britons lay hidden in their dense forests. Then, when it was least expected, they would dart out in their chariots or on horseback and strike at the invaders.

Caesar himself described the tactics of the Britons in his reports to Rome:

> Their manner of fighting from chariots is as follows. First of all they drive in all directions and hurl missiles, and so by the mere terror that the teams inspire and by the noise of the wheels they generally throw the ranks into confusion. When they have worked their way in between the troops of cavalry, they leap down from the chariots and fight on foot. Meanwhile the charioteers retire gradually from the combat and dispose the chariots in such fashion that if the warriors are hard pressed by the host of the enemy, they may have a ready means of retirement to their own side. Thus they show in action the mobility of cavalry and the stability of infantry; and by daily use and practice they become so accomplished that they are ready to gallop their teams down the steepest of slopes without loss of control, to check and turn them in a moment, to run along the pole, stand on the yoke and then, quick as lightning, to dart back into the chariot.

Such acrobatics by the Britons must have astonished the Romans and reminded them of their own chariot-racing in Rome.

Roman foraging parties, searching the countryside for grain and other food, were ambushed and killed. Meanwhile the bad weather was setting in. Gales lashed the sea and Caesar's galleys were badly battered. The ships carrying the Roman cavalry had at last come in sight of land, but a furious storm had forced them back and they had returned to Gaul.

Caesar was in a difficult position. Twelve of his ships were badly damaged and he could not use them to take his troops back to Gaul. He had not brought the provisions and equipment necessary to see them through a winter in Britain. Hurriedly he repaired the damaged ships and left Britain before the summer ended.

Back in Gaul, Caesar spent the winter preparing his next invasion of Britain. This time he assembled an enormous fleet of 800 ships. He was determined to subdue the Britons and sell them into slavery. There were also the valuable tin mines in the south-west of the country that would bring new wealth to Rome. In the spring of 54 B.C., his fleet landed in Kent. This time there were no Britons to resist the Romans. The Britons had sighted this huge armada approaching their shores and had decided for the time being to wait and see.

Caesar pressed on through the countryside. Now and again a party of Britons would attack on chariots, but the Romans proved too powerful for them. Caesar never pursued the enemy once he had shaken them off. There were too many bogs and swamps and dark forests to get lost in.

It was impossible to fight an enemy who kept popping up all of a sudden and then just as quickly disappearing. Caesar decided to try to form an alliance with some of the local chieftains. Some accepted his offer, and he was able, with their help, to crush others who refused. Meanwhile those Britons determined to resist the Romans had appointed a king called Cassivellaunus as their leader. Cassivellaunus ruled a region north of the River Thames and had a fort at a place named Catuvellauni. Caesar reached the fort and seized it after a battle. Later the Romans built their city of Verulamium on the site, near the present-day St. Albans. After their battle, the Romans took some hostages. These were important prisoners who would be killed if the Britons broke their promises to the Romans. These promises involved paying Rome tributes. But Britain was so far away that it was not worth Rome's while

Model showing the construction of a Roman fort. (Museum of Roman Civilization, Rome)

to send an army to collect the tributes when the Britons did break their promise.

Meanwhile there was more trouble brewing in Gaul. A mighty warrior named Vercingetorix had rallied an army of different tribes around him. He was in open rebellion against the Romans. Caesar knew he could no longer stay in Britain. In the late summer he led his troops back to Gaul, never to see Britain again. About a hundred years later more Roman invaders were to come to Britain's shores. This time they stayed for over 400 years and colonized the land, contributing significantly to its development as a great nation.

More Trouble in Gaul

Caesar soon had his hands full when he returned to Gaul from Britain. A new wave of rebellion against the Romans was sweeping the land. The leader of the Gauls, the young nobleman called Vercingetorix, had united the tribes. He held out the exciting prospect of driving the Romans out of the land. Most exciting of all, Vercingetorix planned to invade Italy and perhaps even capture Rome.

Gallic coin, with the head of Vercingetorix.

Caesar immediately set out to stamp out the rebellion. In a series of battles he drove the enemy westwards across Gaul. The retreating rebels burned everything behind them that could be useful to the Romans — houses, villages, and crops. The Gauls finally found themselves at the town of Bourges, in the heart of the country. It was a difficult place to attack. It stood in the middle of a marshy region, with many rivers and streams that were difficult to cross. The town itself was well fortified with walls and gates.

When the Roman army reached Bourges its engineers built a huge ramp 90 metres long and rising to a height of 21 metres. It was like a colossal wedge with the thick end placed against the walls of Bourges. It was the Roman plan to rush up the slope of the ramp and pass over the walls. But the Gauls still had some tricks up their sleeves. During the night they dug tunnels under the town walls and came out on the other side near the wedge. Then, using pitch and tallow, they set fire to the ramp.

The Romans frantically began to try to put the fire out. As fast as they put out the flames more Gauls sneaked out and added more pitch and tallow to keep the blaze going. Eventually the Romans beat off the Gallic fire-raisers and saved the ramp.

On the next day the rain poured down. The Gauls never expected the Romans to launch an attack in such bad weather.

They had not allowed for Caesar's liking for surprise attacks. The Romans rushed up the ramp through the downpour and swarmed into Bourges. The people inside panicked and tried to escape through the narrow doors of the town. They swarmed together in a solid mass and the Romans slaughtered them.

The Gauls hastily withdrew eastwards to Alesia, near present-day Dijon. After some more battles with Caesar's troops, Vercingetorix led his troops into Alesia for protection. Alesia was an even tougher stronghold than Bourges. It stood on a lofty hill commanding a view of the plain, which stretched for about 5 km. towards the surrounding hills. It seemed impossible to capture it except by starving out its 80,000 defenders in a long siege.

Caesar did not like sieges. He ordered his engineers to build a turf wall round the foot of the hill. When it was finished it was 14·5 km. in circumference. The Roman engineers also placed booby traps along the wall. These included pits with huge spikes inside them and logs with iron hooks to catch the legs of any Gauls who tried to escape from the beleaguered fortress.

The worried Gauls kept attacking the Romans as they built their wall. During one of these attacks a party of Gallic horsemen succeeded in breaking through the Roman ranks. They immediately galloped off as fast as they could to bring help from the neighbouring regions.

Caesar realized he was now in danger of being attacked from two sides. He immediately ordered a second wall to be built just outside the first one. The second wall was 21 km. in circumference.

When the Gauls launched their double attack they numbered 250,000 men. The Romans were protected on two sides by their fortifications. But the battle was a bitter one. The Romans drove back wave after wave of the enemy warriors. Caesar himself, dressed in a billowing scarlet cloak, stood in the thick of the fighting, shouting encouragement to his men.

Ruins of Glanum, a city in south-eastern Gaul, captured by Caesar's army.

The battle went on until the evening. Then the Roman cavalry came out and put the enemy to flight.

It was all over with Vercingetorix. On the following day he made his way to the Roman lines. Silently he walked up to Caesar and laid his weapons down at the Roman commander's feet in a token of surrender.

Alesia was the last great battle in the Roman conquest of Gaul. It had been nine years since Caesar left Rome. Now he wanted to return to the city of his birth. But much had changed in Rome. The patricians had become alarmed by the great victories of Caesar. They feared he would return and seize power from them. Even Pompey, who had married Caesar's daughter Julia, was bitterly jealous. The patricians began to plot against Caesar, and Pompey went over to their side.

Civil War

The patricians dreaded Caesar's return to Rome. They had refused his request to extend the period of his command of the army. In the beginning they had made him commander for five years. Later, as his victories grew, they had prolonged this by another five years. But now the great general was coming back to Rome. If he was allowed to keep his soldiers, things could turn dangerous.

'He will seize Rome and take power,' the patricians muttered to one another, 'and then it will be the end for us.'

So when Caesar asked for his command to be extended for a second time, the patricians had refused. They had even asked him to lay down his arms and surrender his command.

The Rubicon, at Savignano, near Rimini. Although only a small stream, the Rubicon was important because it marked the boundary between Cisalpine Gaul and the Roman state.

It was the year 49 B.C., and Caesar had reached a river, called the Rubicon, near Rimini in eastern Italy. The Rubicon was little more than a stream. But it was an extremely important landmark. It marked the boundary with Cisalpine Gaul, and Caesar could not cross it with his army without the permission of the Senate. He sent messengers to Rome to obtain this permission. Some time later, the messengers returned with the Senate's answer:

'You must not cross the Rubicon. The Senate also commands you to lay down your arms and disband your army.'

'And what if I don't?' he demanded.

'Then you will be declared an outlaw and put to death,' the messengers replied.

Caesar's answer to this ultimatum was swift. On the night of 11 January he took his troops across the Rubicon. It was an act of treason. It was also an act that started a civil war in which Roman fought against Roman throughout the provinces. It made

The Senate was the most ancient and respected organ of the government in Rome. Caesar filled it with his supporters, but it was in the Senate that he was assassinated in 44 B.C.

the two former allies, Caesar and Pompey, into sworn enemies.

From that day the phrase "to cross the Rubicon" has meant to do something final, like "burning one's boats".

Caesar had an army of only 1,500 men when he crossed the river. But he met no resistance and soon he had captured a number of towns. Many of the people on his road to Rome joined the ranks of his army.

The patricians became extremely frightened. Rumours buzzed through Rome that Caesar was bringing a horde of wild Gallic tribesmen with him. These stories sent shivers down the backs of the Romans. They remembered the old stories of how the Gauls had burned down their city three centuries before.

The patricians asked Pompey to stop Caesar. Pompey, however, had no wish to fight in Rome. He took his troops out of the city and marched them south to Brundisium, the present-day city of Brindisi. Pompey's action increased the general panic. Shops closed. People hoarded food and money, and business almost came to a standstill.

Caesar reached Rome and learned that Pompey had gone south. He immediately went in pursuit. When he reached Brundisium he saw the last of Pompey's army sailing out of the harbour, bound for Greece.

Julius Caesar. Egyptian bust representing Caesar as a Pharaoh. (Barracco Museum, Rome)

Caesar hurried back to Rome. He had himself made dictator for 11 days and tackled the economic problems of the city. He passed laws punishing people who hoarded money. Other measures restored confidence, and business began to return to normal.

Meanwhile the supporters of Pompey and the patricians were seizing power throughout the provinces. Caesar went off to Spain and regained control of the situation there. The next task was to deal with Pompey. Pompey had an army of 36,000 legionaries, 7,000 cavalrymen, 3,000 archers, and 1,200 slingers. There was also a fleet of 300 ships laden with military equipment and provisions.

Caesar's army numbered 30,000 men. But they were the toughest troops of Rome after their campaigns in Gaul, Spain, and Britain. The army left for Greece, slipping through Pompey's blockade in the Adriatic Sea. Shortly after landing, they captured some small towns. But Pompey moved his troops swiftly, and succeeded in preventing Caesar from capturing the important city of Dyrrachium.

Later, Mark Antony, a friend of Caesar, arrived with more troops and the campaign began to unfold. Caesar's plan was to force Pompey and his troops back to the sea. Pompey saw this, and adopted a trick to divert Caesar. Pompey's scheme was to send out spies disguised as deserters. When the spies reached Caesar they said to him: 'We have decided to leave Pompey and join your side. We can help you to capture Dyrrachium.'

Surprisingly, Caesar did not see through this treachery. He followed the spies to Dyrrachium, and when they came near to the city he and his troops were suddenly caught in an ambush by Pompey and his soldiers. Caesar and his troops were routed. Caesar himself escaped death by inches.

In the summer of 48 B.C. the two armies faced each other on the plain of Pharsalus. Pompey hesitated. He was reluctant to shed the blood of his fellow-Romans. But Caesar was ruthless and he forced his enemy into battle. The battle ended in a crushing victory for Caesar. Pompey escaped from the field and sailed for Egypt, hotly pursued by Caesar.

Three days later Caesar arrived in Egypt. He was met by a group of people, one of whom carried something covered by a cloth. When they took the cloth away, there was Pompey's blood-stained head.

Caesar wept. His quarrel with Pompey had been purely political, and he had liked him as a person. The Egyptians had killed the Roman general to win Caesar's favour.

SSENDO CESARE in lumbardia asouernare como di sopra hauemo duto molte + nouelle aluy erano referite per Lettere di Labieno anchora certificato fue tuti li belgi che la tercia parte di gallia como c dimonstrato otteneno contra el populo di Roma noua conuuratione incominciare e gli ostadi fra loro inseme dare Le cagione di tale cō

Caesar receiving the submission of Gallic chiefs. Title page of a medieval edition of Caesar's *Gallic War*.

In Egypt, Caesar found a civilization older even than that of Rome. The façade of the Great Temple of Abu Simbel, in the Nile Valley.

At that time the throne of Egypt was shared by the beautiful young queen Cleopatra and her brother Ptolemy. Each wanted to be the sole ruler, and their advisers and supporters plotted and struggled against each other. Caesar took a liking to the beautiful young queen and decided to support her. More battles followed, and Caesar once more narrowly escaped death. In the end Cleopatra came to the throne, and her enemies were banished.

In 47 B.C. Caesar decided to return to Rome. But first he went to Asia Minor, where trouble had broken out. Mithridates, that old enemy of Rome, was dead. But his son Pharnaces was following in his footsteps. The young king was busily stealing Roman territory and adding it to his own kingdom. When Caesar arrived in Asia Minor, the hot-headed Pharnaces immediately attacked him at a place called Zela. Caesar won the battle. Pharnaces fled and was later killed.

This engagement resulted in Caesar's briefest and most famous dispatch. It read simply: *Veni, vidi, vici*, meaning "I came, I saw, I conquered".

Caesar returned to Rome in the summer. In the following year he was elected Consul once more, and he administered the affairs of state for some time. But the fighting was not over. Some of Caesar's enemies had gone to northern Africa and allied themselves with Juba, king of Numidia, a region now forming part of Libya and Tunisia. Juba had already been successful in a battle against some of Caesar's supporters.

Caesar hurried out to Africa. Within a few weeks he overcame

(Below left) Cleopatra, the beautiful queen of Egypt, with whom Caesar fell in love. (Below right) Mark Antony, who supported Caesar against Pompey.

his enemies. The great general had now heaped up victories in Gaul, Spain, Asia, and Africa, and Rome prepared the greatest welcome in its history for him.

Not one, but three triumphs were given. The city was garlanded with flowers, and incense burned fragrantly from hundreds of altars.

The processions that passed through the city glittered with all the plundered treasures taken in Caesar's campaigns. Barbarian kings and chieftains captured in battle were brought out from the dungeons and displayed to the mobs. One of these prisoners was the once-great Vercingetorix. It was his last sight of the blazing sun and the clear blue sky, for he was later put to death.

Caesar gave a banquet for 20,000 poor people. Each guest was given gifts of wheat, money, and oil to light their lamps at night in their homes. Great games were held in the stadiums. An artificial lake was created, and a mock battle between ships was fought out before thousands of delighted spectators.

Rome had never seen anything like it. The historian Suetonius wrote:

> Such a throng flocked to all those shows that many visitors to the city had to sleep in tents pitched in the streets. The crowd was often so large that many people, including two senators, were crushed to death.

Everywhere the name of Caesar was on everybody's lips. It seemed that he reached the loftiest peak of might and fame. And yet it was all to end soon in tragedy and bloodshed.

Caesar, to the people, was now a god. Everywhere statues to him were erected. Temples were called after him. The month of Quintilis was renamed Julius in his honour. The name July today still records his fame. He was made dictator for ten years. Rome was his.

The patricians were filled with dread. They feared that Caesar, so idolized by the common people, would squeeze them out of

A Gallic soldier taken prisoner by the Romans. Relief from a Roman triumphal arch at Carpentras, in southern France.

Ruins of Caesar's Forum in Rome, near the *Forum Romanum*. Its building was ordered by Caesar.

existence. Meanwhile Caesar became busy passing new laws. He introduced new and better ways of collecting taxes. He attacked those patricians who loved to flaunt their wealth, and forbade them to do so. For those soldiers who had fought faithfully under his command he set aside land and jobs.

One of his major achievements was to change the Roman calendar. This had only 355 days and did not match with the length of the four seasons. Caesar extended it to 365 and a quarter days. Caesar also had ambitious plans to drain marshes and turn them into fertile farmlands. He wanted to build a road over the snow-capped Apennine mountains that run down the middle of Italy and link Rome with the Adriatic Sea. His other schemes included deepening the harbour near Rome, and changing the course of the River Tiber to control its waters. He also planned to build magnificent

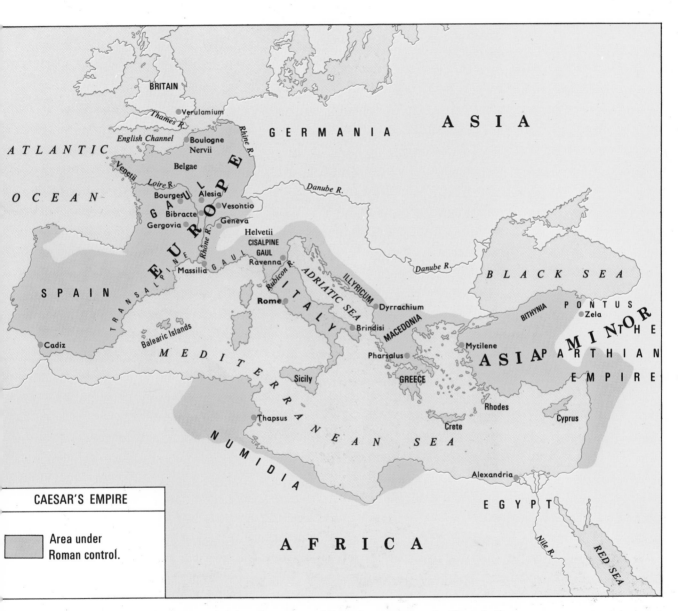

CAESAR'S EMPIRE

Area under
Roman control.

Map showing the extent of Rome's possessions in Caesar's time.

51

Julius Caesar. (Uffizi Gallery, Florence)

libraries and theatres, and more parklands for the Roman citizens.

But the patricians distrusted him deeply.

'Just wait,' they said. 'He will not be satisfied with being dictator. He will want to be a king next.'

The Ides of March

There had been some rather disturbing signs. Caesar refused to observe the custom and stand up whenever he was addressed in the Senate.

'He thinks he is mightier than the rest of us,' the patricians said.

One day a crown was found placed on one of his statues. The crown was quickly removed. Caesar accused his enemies of having put it there to cause him trouble, but many did not believe this. On 26 January, 45 B.C. Caesar was returning from the games. Some demonstrators suddenly rushed out and greeted him as *Rex* meaning *king*. The demonstrators were immediately arrested. Caesar replied: 'I am not *king* but *Caesar*!'

In the Latin this was *Non sum Rex sed Caesar*. But the patricians pointed out that *Rex* (like the English word "King") could be a surname and said Caesar had not really rejected the title of monarch. They also pointed out that Caesar ordered it to be placed in the records that he had been greeted as king.

Later there was another strange event. It was the feast of Lupercalia. Caesar sat on the gilded throne he was entitled to in his new position of power. In front of him passed a procession of priests. Mark Antony went up to Caesar with a coronet and offered it to him. The crowd groaned as Caesar hesitated.

In his play *Julius Caesar*, William Shakespeare described the scene through the character of Casca, one of Caesar's enemies:

I saw Mark Antony offer him a crown...and as I told you he put it by once: but, for all that, to my thinking, he would fain have had it. Then he offered it to him again; then he put it by again; but, to my thinking, he was very loath to lay his fingers off it. And then he offered it the third time; he put it the third time by: and still, as he refused it, the rabblement hooted and clapped their chapped hands and threw up their sweaty night-caps and uttered such a deal of stinking breath because Caesar refused the crown...

What was Caesar doing, the patricians wondered. Was he trying to find out what the people thought about his becoming king? Or did he really mean to refuse the crown? The patricians themselves had no doubt. Caesar was too ambitious. He wanted to become king. The Roman republic was in danger.

The conspirators gathered together. There were about 60 of them. They included Cassius, who had fought for Pompey at the Battle of Pharsalus. Caesar had pardoned him after the victory, but he did not trust him. There was Brutus, a dear friend of Caesar, and Caesar would never have suspected him of treachery. But Brutus, much as he loved Caesar, hated the idea of a king ruling Rome.

The decision was made that Caesar must be killed. The assassination was to take place in the Senate. The date was set as the Ides of March — 15 March in the Roman calendar.

During the night before, Caesar's wife Calpurnia tossed and turned in her bed. Her sleep was tormented by nightmares. She kept dreaming that her husband had been murdered. The next morning she pleaded with him not to go to the Senate. He laughed at her fears but delayed his departure.

Meanwhile the conspirators waited at the Senate. Each of them had a long sharp dagger hidden beneath his robes. When Caesar did not appear they became anxious and one of them was sent to Caesar's house to find out what was wrong. When he heard about Calpurnia's dreams he laughed and said: 'Surely you don't believe in such silly things.' Calpurnia remained nervous, but Caesar agreed with the messenger that her fears were groundless.

Caesar set forth. As he approached the Senate he spotted a soothsayer, one of the many fortune tellers who claimed they could see into the future, in the crowd. This soothsayer had once warned Caesar: 'Beware the Ides of March!'

Marcus Junius Brutus (c85–42 B.C.) took part in Caesar's murder. He loved Caesar, but feared that Caesar would destroy the republic.

'The Ides of March have come,' Caesar called out to the man. 'Aye, but not gone,' the soothsayer replied grimly.

Caesar strode into the Senate building. Somebody stopped his friend Mark Antony and Caesar entered the debating chamber alone. He sat down in his seat and was immediately surrounded

Gaius Julius Caesar Octavianus, known as Augustus. Julius Caesar's heir and successor, he was emperor from 27 B.C. to A.D. 14 — the Golden Age of Rome. Statue by Cleomenes. (Louvre, Paris)

by a crowd of Senators. One man, Tillius Cimber, threw himself to his knees before Caesar.

'Caesar,' he begged, 'I beseech you to let my brother return from exile.'

Caesar told Cimber to move back. Instead, the man clutched at Caesar's toga and pulled it downwards. Caesar's neck and chest were exposed. The next moment Casca came up behind Caesar and stabbed him in the neck. Immediately the rest of the plotters were lunging at him with their knives. Caesar fought back desperately. Soon his white robes were stained red with blood. As he staggered, back, he saw through misty eyes Brutus approach him with a dagger in his hand.

Et tu, Brute, Caesar whispered. 'Even you, Brutus.'

The great man then fell to the floor dead, his body gashed with more than 30 stab wounds.

The citizens of Rome were stunned by the murder. Then they plunged the city into riots, and the bloodshed continued for weeks.

Mark Antony then formed a triumvirate with Octavian, Caesar's nephew, and Lepidus, who had served as Consul with Caesar. Their first aim was to avenge the assassination. Brutus and Cassius killed themselves in 42 B.C., just before they were defeated by Antony. Many Romans involved in the drama died in the years that followed, including Antony.

Octavian survived and became the first Emperor of Rome, with the name of Augustus. The republic had died with Caesar, but the great Roman empire emerged from the tragedy, an empire which owed its existence to Caesar.

Important Dates